D1461413

Phil Dampier has been a journalist for 30 years. For a decade he worked for *The Sun*, first as west-country correspondent, when he covered the 1983 General Election, and then as royal reporter. As a freelance writer for the last 16 years his articles, mainly about the royal family, have been published in newspapers and magazines worldwide.

He has always had an abiding interest in politics, but is fearful that recent Prime Ministers have made the office too presidential. He is also concerned that modern day career politicians no longer seem to have any convictions.

'I hope this book helps to show that all Prime Ministers are temporary custodians of the office and need to respond more to the public's wishes,' he said.

He lives in Kent with his partner Ann.

Ashley Walton has been a journalist all his working life. He began at 16, as an articled junior reporter in Nuneaton, where his most important role was making tea. He worked his way up via regional weekly and evening newspapers and arrived in Fleet Street in the early 1970s at the *Daily Express*, where he stayed to take on various jobs over the next 23 years.

As a young reporter in Camberley he covered the funeral of Sir Winston Churchill for a special pull out edition. When Mrs Thatcher was elected leader of the Conservatives he was the first reporter to get an impromptu interview with her when she invited him into her Chelsea home. Later he covered her first election campaign, travelling with her round Britain.

As royal correspondent on the *Daily Express* he met many politicians, diplomats and heads of state on official worldwide tours with the Queen. 'Royal reporting, particularly that involving the diplomacy of foreign state visits by the Queen, was always politically based,' he said. 'I have always had a fascination for the quote that becomes part of history.'

Ashley lives in Hertfordshire with his wife Joan. They have two sons, Nic and Oliver.

By the same authors:

Duke of Hazard, The Wit and Wisdom of Prince Philip, The Book Guild, 2006

What's in the Queen's Handbag, The Book Guild, 2007

THE WIT AND WISDOM OF BRITISH PRIME MINISTERS

Phil Dampier and
Ashley Walton

Book Guild Publishing
Sussex, England

The authors are grateful to Paul Cook,
London Account Manager of
Amalgamated Book Services,
who gave us the idea for this title.

First published in Great Britain in 2008 by
The Book Guild Ltd
Pavilion View
19 New Road
Brighton BN1 1UF

Second Printing 2008

Typesetting in Garamond by
Keyboard Services, Luton, Bedfordshire

Printed and bound in the UK by CPI Mackays, Chatham ME5 8TD

A catalogue record for this book is available from
The British Library

ISBN 978 1 84624 222 9

CONTENTS

INTRODUCTION

After ten years of Tony Blair, Gordon Brown became Britain's 52nd Prime Minister in June 2007. Only time will tell if this dour Scotsman and former Chancellor of the Exchequer can shake off his dull image and compete with Blair's brilliant communication skills. If he does, he will follow in a fine tradition of incisive wit and wisdom displayed by the 50 men, and one woman, who have occupied 10 Downing Street in the last four centuries.

They were not, it has to be said, all great orators. One was a crook, others reckless womanisers, and a few were just plain dull. But the majority were the great wits and visionaries of their day, and many of their musings and mutterings have stood the test of time and are still in common usage today: 'Bob's your uncle' began when one PM called Robert made his nephew Home Secretary; 'All men have their price' was coined by Sir Robert Walpole, the first PM; and 'Publish and be damned' originated when the Duke of Wellington was threatened with blackmail.

Some PMs were masters of vicious put-downs. Like Disraeli who wrote to an aspiring author: 'Many thanks for your book, I shall lose no time in reading it.' And

Churchill who retorted to a woman who accused him of being drunk: 'I may be drunk, Madam, but in the morning I shall be sober and you will still be ugly.'

This hilarious romp though nearly 300 years of classic quotes shows our Premiers in a new light. Funny, fascinating and informative, this potted history shows that hundreds of Prime Ministers' witticisms really were 'First among equals'.

THE GEORGIAN PRIME MINISTERS: POETS, POLITICS AND POTENTATES

- George I was halfway through his 13-year reign when Walpole emerged as his first minister in 1721.

- The great architect of St Paul's Cathedral Sir Christopher Wren died in 1723 as the age of enlightenment began to dawn.

○ In 1733 John Kay invented the Flying Shuttle, the first great textile machine, and the industrial revolution began to transform British cities, while the Empire expanded rapidly.

○ Conflict was never far away in the 18th century with the War of Jenkins Ear between Britain and Spain in 1739, and George II became the last monarch to command arms in the field when the French were defeated at Dettingen in 1743.

○ With George III on the throne from 1760, John Wesley spread his Methodist message.

○ In France, the great philosopher Jean-Jacques Rousseau became a forerunner of the romantic movement with his cry for 'liberty, equality and fraternity'. His views helped to inspire the French Revolution and the founding fathers of the United States, as America fought for, and won, independence.

○ The Whigs and the Tories slowly evolved as the world's first political parties, with most of the 18th century dominated by the former after the latter were tainted by support for the failed Jacobite rebellions of 1715 and 1745.

○ While Lancelot 'Capability' Brown laid out his magnificent gardens at Blenheim Palace, Kew and Stowe, man of letters Samuel Johnson was at the centre of London literary life.

2

o As Canaletto captured London and Venice on canvas, Gainsborough, Hogarth and Reynolds created their own masterpieces, and Stubbs brought horses to life with his paintings.

o As the 18th century bowed out, Jane Austen began writing her novels full of restrained passion.

o Admiral Horatio Nelson died a heroic death at the 1805 Battle of Trafalgar.

o And while Napoleon conquered Europe, the slave trade was abolished in 1807.

SIR ROBERT WALPOLE, EARL OF ORFORD (1676–1745)

Years in office: 1721–42
Party: Whig
Age when first became PM: 44
Time at Number 10: 20 years and 314 days
Nicknames: 'Sir Blustering' and 'Screen Master General'

Walpole was a great Prime Minister but also a total crook. He was the first to live and work at Downing Street and the longest serving Prime Minister, although he did not use that title. As MP for King's Lynn he craved power and used it with great skill, and a little bribery and corruption, to get rich in a career of illicit money-making deals. Unmasked, he could have gone to the gallows, but instead was sent to the Tower of London where he had a suite of rooms and a personal chef. He served just six months before being released and was immediately re-elected as MP. Then he crawled his way up the greasy pole to Number 10. He lived high and indulged his wife's very expensive tastes. He was said to have a 'vulgar' love of expense without any true notion of magnificence. He was so vulgar that he even wore his glittering stars and embroidered badges of office when out walking his dogs.

He also had an expensive taste in extramarital affairs, keeping a string of mistresses. When his wife Catherine died, he married his favourite mistress, Maria Skerett who was 26 years his junior. Known for being frank and

4

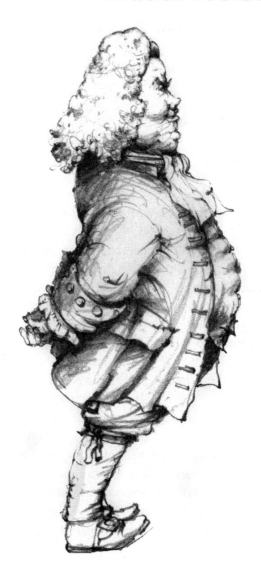

hearty and very clever at using political subtlety and charm, he died deeply in debt, losing everything by living beyond his means. Died aged 68.

The Wit and Wisdom

On the declaration of war with Spain: 'They now ring the bells, but they will soon wring their hands.'

Of fellow politicians: 'All those men have their price.'

On the War of Polish Succession in which the English had refused to take part: 'There are fifty thousand men slain this year in Europe, and not one Englishman.'

On the great historical canon: 'I do not read history for that I know to be false.'

He coined the phrase: 'The balance of power.'

On himself: 'I am no saint, no Spartan, no reformer.'

When he was dying (from a lacerated bladder) he told his doctor, who was called Ranby, that he wanted his body cut open. 'Good God, my Lord, don't talk of that,' cried the doctor. 'Nay, sir,' replied Walpole. 'It will not be until I am dead and then I shall not feel it nor you neither.'

SPENCER COMPTON, EARL OF WILMINGTON (1673–1743)

Years in office: 1742–3
Party: Whig
Age when first became PM: 69
Time at Number 10: 1 year, 136 days

A bachelor who was said to have fathered a string of illegitimate children, Spencer Compton was considered only to be a 'stop gap' PM. He turned out to be an undistinguished leader. Famous only for being a gourmet. Died aged 70.

The Wit and Wisdom

To the Duke of Newcastle: 'Sir, you have a right to speak, but the house has a right to judge whether they hear you.'

HENRY PELHAM (1694–1754)

Years in office: 1743–54
Party: Whig
Age when first became PM: 48
Time at Number 10: 10 years, 191 days
Nickname: 'King Henry the Ninth'

He's the man who gave the orders to put down Bonnie Prince Charlie's rebellion, dealing severely with Jacobite sympathisers. He came from a *Dallas*-style powerful political dynasty and his brother followed him into Number 10. He died in office because he ate too much and exercised too little. His love of fine wines and over-indulgence is still honoured at Oxford where the prestigious drinking club 'The Sir Henry Pelham Gentleman's Sporting Society' is named in his honour. Died aged 59.

On the House of Lords: 'Let them alone, they make better speeches for us than we can make for ourselves.'

'The House of Commons is a great unwieldy body, which requires great art and some cordial to keep it loyal.'

THOMAS PELHAM-HOLLES, DUKE OF NEWCASTLE (1693–1768)

Years in office: 1754–6 and 1757–62
Party: Whig
Age when first became PM: 60
Time in Office: 7 years, 205 days
Nickname: 'Hubble Bubble' because he was so energetic and always on the go.

He followed his brother Henry Pelham as Prime Minister. Not a great man but an industrious and very moral one. He was a hypochondriac, forever worrying about his health. He led Britain into the disastrous Seven Years' War with France, which drained the nation and led to his own downfall. Unlike many modern Prime Ministers, he sought neither fame nor wealth after leaving office. He twice refused a pension and was left £300,000 poorer than when he entered Number 10. Died aged 75.

The Wit and Wisdom

'I shall not ... think the demands of the people a rule of conduct, nor shall I even fear to incur their resentment in the prosecution of their interest. I shall never flatter their passions to obtain their favour, or gratify their revenge for fear of contempt.'

WILLIAM CAVENDISH, DUKE OF DEVONSHIRE (1720–64)

Years in office: 1756–7
Party: Whig
Age when first became PM: 36
Time at Number 10: 225 days

Tall, imposing, and said to be the best-looking man in London, but his brief time as Prime Minister was lacklustre and riddled with domestic problems. He was a reluctant PM, manoeuvred into office by King George II. He resigned after just 225 days in office and died eight years later aged just 44. He married 16-year-old Charlotte, although he was eleven years her senior. She bore him four children and died aged just 23.

The Wit and Wisdom

'Every king must make use of human means to attain human ends or his affairs will go to ruin.'

JOHN STUART, EARL OF BUTE (1713–92)

Years in office: 1762–3
Party: Tory
Age when first became PM: 49
Time at Number 10: 317 days
Nickname: 'Jack Boot'

He was the first Scottish-born PM, which made him extremely unpopular with the English who mistrusted the Scots. He was tall, slim and very handsome, and was projected into office after only three years in Parliament because of his friendship with King George III. But he had to suffer countless verbal, written and even physical assaults over his Scottishness. He fathered 11 children in 18 years to his wife Mary who he married when she was just 18. Died aged 78.

The Wit and Wisdom

During a debate on cider tax he said: 'A noble duke knows the difficulty to choose proper taxes.'

GEORGE GRENVILLE (1712–70)

Years in office: 1763–5
Party: Whig
Age when first became PM: 50
Time at Number 10: 2 years, 85 days
Nickname: 'The Gentle Shepherd'

Tactless and boring, the man who is credited with beginning the unrest in the colonies, which led to the War of Independence and the formation of the United States. King George III couldn't stand him and eventually sacked him, a rare event in British politics. Tried to make himself popular by cutting taxes at home to the expense of the colonies, fomenting the start of unrest in America. Even his nickname was a reference to him being a bore. He kept changing his mind about taxation in the House of Commons, and the opposition began whistling 'The Gentle Shepherd', a popular tune at the time about an indecisive man. Died aged 58.

The Wit and Wisdom

'A wise government knows how to enforce with temper or to conciliate with dignity. But a weak one is odious in the former and contemptible in the latter.'

CHARLES WENTWORTH, MARQUESS OF ROCKINGHAM (1730–82)

Years in office: 1765–6 and 1782
Party: Whig
Age when first became PM: 36
Time at Number 10: 1 year, 113 days

Wealthy but very naïve when it came to the dirty business of politics. Loved betting and horse racing. Sacked by King George III. Died aged 52.

The Wit and Wisdom

'Englishmen, whatever their local situation may be, know no obedience to anything but the law.'

THE EARL OF CHATHAM, WILLIAM PITT 'THE ELDER' (1708–78)

Years in office: 1766–8
Party: Whig
Age when first became PM: 57
Time at Number 10: 2 years, 76 days
Nickname: 'The Great Commoner'

One of the most striking political figures of the 18th century. He was aloof, a solitary figure who, according to a member of his family, 'lived and died without a friend'. Tall, with the eye of a hawk, aggressive with commanding presence. Credited with the birth of the British Empire which made him very popular with the people, hence his nickname. Died aged 69.

The Wit and Wisdom

'The poorest man may in his cottage bid defiance to all the forces of the Crown. It may be frail, its roof may shake, the wind may blow through it, the storm may enter, the rain may enter, but the King of England cannot enter!'

'Confidence is a plant of slow growth in an aged bosom. Youth is the season of credulity.'

14

'Unlimited power is apt to corrupt the minds of those who possess it.'

'There is something behind the throne greater than the King himself.'

'You cannot conquer America.'

'The parks are the lungs of London.'

'Our watchword is security.'

AUGUSTUS HENRY FITZROY, DUKE OF GRAFTON (1735–1811)

Years in office: 1767–70
Party: Whig
Age when first became PM: 33
Time at Number 10: 1 year, 106 days
Nicknames: 'Royal Oak' and 'Turf Macaroni' because he loved horse racing.

Shy, but with a notorious wandering eye for the ladies. So busy he often fell asleep during Cabinet meetings. He scandalised society with his philandering, constantly unfaithful to his wife who in turn was unfaithful to him. Resigned after attacks on him by newspapers. Died aged 75.

The Wit and Wisdom

'Wisdom is at no time more conspicuous, nor more amiable, than in the acknowledgement of error.'

LORD NORTH (1730–92)

Years in office: 1770–82
Party: Tory
Age when first became PM: 37
Time at Number 10: 12 years, 58 days
Nickname: 'Boreas' (The North Wind)

A disastrous Prime Minister. Although hard-working, he made terrible tactical errors in dragging Britain into the War of Independence. He pleaded in vain with King George III to allow him to resign but the King only allowed it after the war had ended, leaving North to take all the blame. He resigned after a vote of no confidence. He once jokingly called himself, his wife and one of their daughters, 'three of the ugliest people in London'. Died aged 60.

The Wit and Wisdom

'Men may be popular without being ambitious. But there is hardly an ambitious man who does not try to be popular.'

WILLIAM PETTY, EARL OF SHELBURNE (1737–1805)

Years in office: 1782–3
Party: Whig
Age when first became PM: 45
Time at Number 10: 266 days
Nicknames: 'Malagrida' and 'The Jesuit in Berkeley Square' (by George III, who didn't trust him)

Petty was seen as devious and untrustworthy. He concluded the Treaty of Paris, giving independence to the new United States and making him a lot of enemies. He was one of the most consistently unpopular Prime Ministers. Died aged 68.

The Wit and Wisdom

'A one thousand acres that can feed one thousand souls is better than ten thousands acres of no more effect.'

'If great cities are naturally apt to remove their seats, I ask which way? I say in the case of London it must be westward. If it follow for hence that the palaces of the greatest men will remove westward, it will also naturally follow that the dwelling of others who depend on them will creep after them.'

'That some are poorer than others ever was and ever will be, and that many are naturally querulous and envious is an evil as old as the world.'

'No man pays double or twice for the same thing for as much as nothing can be spent but once.'

WILLIAM BENTINCK, DUKE OF PORTLAND (1738–1809)

Years in office: 1783 and 1807–9
Party: Whig
Age when first became PM: 44
Time at Number 10: 3 years, 82 days

Tall, dignified and handsome, he may have been, but Bentinck was not considered a worthwhile PM. In his second term of office he was too old and ill to run the government and left his Cabinet to do much as they pleased. Died aged 71.

The Wit and Wisdom

On accepting office the second time: 'My fears are not that the attempt to perform the duty will shorten my life but that I shall neither bodily nor mentally perform as I should.'

WILLIAM PITT 'THE YOUNGER' (1759–1806)

Years in office: 1783–1801 and 1804–6
Party: Tory
Age when first became PM: 24
Time at Number 10: 18 years, 343 days
Nicknames: 'Pitt the Younger' and 'Bottomless Pitt'
(not for the depth of his knowledge, but because he was so thin)

Youngest ever Prime Minister at the helm in one of the most momentous times in history, from the French Revolution and the Napoleonic Wars to the Union with Ireland. Obsessed with politics from the age of seven. A popular ditty at the time went: 'A sight to make all nations stand and stare; a kingdom trusted to a schoolboy's care.' He was advised by his doctor to drink a bottle of port a day to cure his gout. He died from cirrhosis of the liver aged just 46. Fond of pies, he died unmarried and deep in debt.

The Wit and Wisdom

Last words: 'Oh my country! How I love my country!'

Or alternative attributed last words: 'I think I could eat one of Bellamy's veal pies.'

'Pie is the fuel of Britain.'

On the execution of Louis XVI of France: 'On every principle by which men of justice and honour are actuated, it is the foulest and most atrocious deed which the history of the world has yet had occasion to attest.'

'Necessity is the plea for every infringement of human freedom. It is the argument of tyrants, it is the creed of slaves.'

HENRY ADDINGTON (1757–1844)

Years in office: 1801–4
Party: Tory
Age when first became PM: 43
Time at Number 10: 3 years, 54 days
Nickname: 'The Doctor'

He was the royal doctor who treated King George III during one of the King's famous bouts of madness. Known as a very poor speaker. Died aged 86.

The Wit and Wisdom

'In youth, the absence of pleasure is pain, in old age the absence of pain is pleasure.'

'I hate Liberality. Nine times out of ten it is cowardice and the tenth time, lack of principle.'

WILLIAM WYNDAM GRENVILLE, LORD GRENVILLE (1759–1834)

Years in office: 1806–7
Party: Whig
Age when first became PM: 46
Time at Number 10: 1 year, 42 days
Nickname: 'Bogey'

Poor public image, just like earlier Prime Minister George Grenville (his father). Famous for the abolition of slavery. Died aged 74.

The Wit and Wisdom

On his resignation: 'The deed is done and I am again a free man.'

Not a keen politician: 'I can hardly keep wondering at my own folly in thinking it worthwhile to leave my books and garden, even for one day's attendance in the House of Commons.'

THE REGENCY AND BEYOND – WITS, FOPS AND FASHIONISTAS

○ As George III descended into madness, his son the Prince of Wales (later George IV) took over as Prince Regent in 1811.

○ The following year Napoleon's Grand Army was forced to withdraw from Moscow, and Wellington began to get the upper hand in Spain. Napoleon abdicated in 1814 and was banished to Elba, only to escape and meet his 'Waterloo' the following year.

○ The Corn Laws were introduced to keep up prices and protect agriculture from cheap imports.

○ In 1820 George III died and was succeeded by his son, who became known as the 'first gentleman of Europe' for his interest in the arts and architecture.

○ Keats published *Lamia, Isabella, The Eve of St Agnes* and other romantic poems, but he and Shelley both died young in Italy, while the great German composer Beethoven bowed out in 1827.

○ The Industrial Revolution was transforming the landscape, but social and political reform lagged behind. When protestors in Manchester demanded rights, 11 were killed in the 'Peterloo Massacre' of 1819, while a decade later Peel founded the Metropolitan police to keep order in London.

○ The first railway was built between Stockton and Darlington, the Atlantic was crossed by steamship, Morse invented the electric telegraph, and Faraday discovered electromagnetic induction.

○ George IV died in 1830 and was succeeded by his brother William IV who reigned for seven years. The 'Sailor King' did not oppose the 1832 Reform Act, which doubled the number of people who could vote. Democracy was spreading like a virus.

SPENCER PERCEVAL (1762–1812)

Years in office: 1809–12
Party: Tory
Age when first became PM: 46
Time at Number 10: 2 years, 221 days
Nickname: 'Little P'

Only British Prime Minister to have been assassinated (in the lobby of the House of Commons, 11 May, 1812). Father of twelve, six sons, six daughters. Fond of biblical prophecy. Died aged 49.

The Wit and Wisdom

Last words: 'Oh. I have been murdered!'

During a debate on corrupt electoral practice. 'I have nothing to say to the nothing that has been said.'

ROBERT BANKS JENKINSON, EARL OF LIVERPOOL (1770–1828)

Years in office: 1812–27
Party: Tory
Age when first became PM: 42
Time at Number 10: 14 years, 305 days

Stayed in power for nearly 15 years, not through his own talent but by means of changing his views to fit the occasion and by surrounding himself with colleagues more talented and ambitious than himself. Liverpool Street Station is named after him. Died aged 58.

The Wit and Wisdom

'[I consider] the right of election as a public trust, granted not for the benefit of the individual, but for the public good.'

GEORGE CANNING (1770–1827)

Years in office: 1827
Party: Tory
Age when first became PM: 57
Time at Number 10: 119 days
Nicknames: 'The Cicero of the British Senate' and 'The Zany of Debate'

Witty, popular and an excellent public speaker. Born into poverty and married an heiress Joan Scott but always had financial problems. Fought a duel with Castlereagh in 1809. Because he had never fired a pistol before, Canning missed completely. Castlereagh fired, wounding his opponent in the thigh. Died in office from pneumonia aged just 57. He was known as the 'lost leader' because his sudden death gave him no time for achievements in office.

The Wit and Wisdom

On Society: 'Indecision and delays are the parents of failure.'

'The happiness of constant occupation is infinite.'

Canning was fond of verse. This is a coded message he sent to the British ambassador in the Netherlands: 'In matters of commerce the fault of the Dutch is offering too little and asking too much. The French are with equal advantage content, so we'll lay on Dutch bottoms just twenty per cent.'

On himself: 'I can prove anything by statistics, except for the truth.'

Last words: 'Spain and Portugal.'

FREDERICK ROBINSON, VISCOUNT GODERICH (1782–1859)

Years in office: 1827–8
Party: Tory
Age when first became PM: 44
Time at Number 10: 130 days
Nicknames: 'Goody Goderich' and 'The Blubberer'

Emotional and impracticable and certainly not up to the task of controlling his quarrelling Cabinet. He resigned after just four months, achieving nothing. Married to Sarah Hobart, a notorious and neurotic hypochondriac. He died aged 76.

The Wit and Wisdom

'There was no one good thing in this life that had not with it some concomitant evil.'

ARTHUR WELLESLEY, DUKE OF WELLINGTON (1769–1852)

Years in office: 1828–30
Party: Tory
Age when first became PM: 58
Time at Number 10: 2 years, 320 days
Nickname: 'The Iron Duke'

More famous and more popular for his military exploits than his politics. He was totally indifferent to the opinions of others. He fought a duel with Lord Winchilsea in Battersea Park in 1829. The two had fallen out over the granting of almost full civil rights to Catholics, but deliberately missed each other, and honour was satisfied. Gave his name to a humble boot. Died aged 83.

The Wit and Wisdom

Describing his first Cabinet meeting as PM: 'An extraordinary affair. I gave them their orders and they wanted to stay and discuss them.'

On his deathbed after being offered a cup of tea: 'Yes, if you please.'

On his Irish birthright: 'Being born in a stable does not make one a horse.'

On a blackmail threat: 'Publish and be damned!'

On himself: 'The only thing I am afraid of is fear.'

On the first time he went to Parliament: 'I never saw so many shocking bad hats in my life.'

On the Battle of Waterloo: 'The most desperate business I was ever in.'

Talking about his own soldiers: 'I don't know what effect these men will have on the enemy, but by God they frighten me.'

On religions: 'Educate people without religion and you make them but clever devils.'

'The Lord's Prayer contains the sum total of religion and morals.'

EARL GREY (1764–1845)

Years in office: 1830–4
Party: Whig
Age when first became PM: 66
Time at Number 10: 3 years, 229 days

Tall and strikingly handsome, he was responsible for the start of radical election reform and the abandonment of slavery in the British Empire. Another politician who had a home hobby, he fathered 17 children (one illegitimate). He was best known for his liking for a particular brand of tea flavoured with bergamot oil. 'Earl Grey' is still very popular today. Died aged 81.

The Wit and Wisdom

'The only way with newspaper attacks is, as the Irish say, "to keep never minding". This has been my practice through life.'

'Politics is a pursuit, which I detest, which interferes with all my private comfort, and which I only sigh for an opportunity of abandoning decidedly and for ever.'

WILLIAM LAMB,
VISCOUNT MELBOURNE (1779–1848)

Years in office: 1834 and 1835–41
Party: Whig
Age when first became PM: 55
Time at Number 10: 6 years, 255 days

He had two lives: one, the cuckolded husband in the most scandalous affair of the 19th century; the other, as senior statesman and personal friend to Queen Victoria. His wife, Lady Caroline Ponsonby, had a very public affair with Lord Byron, the talk of Britain in 1812. Died aged 69.

The Wit and Wisdom

'It is impossible that anyone can feel the being out of Parliament more keenly for me than I feel it for myself. It is actually cutting the throat. It is depriving me of the great object of my life.'

To a bishop who asked him to attend church twice in one day: 'Once is orthodox, twice is puritanical.'

After enduring an evangelical sermon: ' Things have come to a pretty pass when religion is allowed to invade the sphere of private life.'

'My exoteric doctrine is that if you entertain any doubt, it is safest to take the unpopular side in the first instance. Transit from the unpopular is easy. But from the popular to the unpopular is so steep and rugged that it is impossible to maintain it.'

'God help the Minister that meddles with art!'

'Damn it! Another Bishop dead! I believe they die to vex me.'

To a politician who said he would support Lamb when he was in the right: 'What I want is men who will support me when I am in the wrong.'

GREAT VICTORIANS:
EMPIRE, INDUSTRY
AND INVENTION

o Queen Victoria's extraordinary 63-year reign saw
  remarkable men and women achieve greatness in many
  different fields.

o As the Empire expanded, victories and discoveries
  abroad were matched by achievements at home,
  creating much of our modern infrastructure that
  we take for granted, including railways, roads and
  sewers.

o Britain became the 'workshop of the world', with factories churning out goods, although conditions for workers were often appalling.

o Glasgow produced a quarter of all the ships built on the planet. And brilliant engineers like Isambard Kingdom Brunel got things done by sheer determination and will. He built the Great Western Railway, ships like the *Great Western* and *Great Britain*, and the Clifton Suspension Bridge in Bristol.

o Others constructed the Forth Bridge and the Manchester Ship Canal, while the Suez Canal was opened in 1869.

o In 1861, as America descended into a bloody civil war, Victoria's beloved husband Prince Albert died and she wore black for the rest of her life.

o While Charles Darwin wrote *The Origin of Species*, others were looking forward, inventing the telephone, motorcar and electricity.

o Improvements in communications, with the Penny Post, newspapers and magazines, meant people became famous for their feats: Florence Nightingale, the 'Lady of the Lamp' who cared for wounded soldiers in The Crimea; David Livingstone, who discovered the Victoria Falls, fought against slavery and was thought lost in Africa, only to be traced by Stanley; and William Booth, who founded the Salvation Army.

○ Dickens and Tennyson, the great novelist and poet of their age, mirrored Victorian society in their epic works.

○ Oscar Wilde was the great wit of his era, imprisoned for his homosexuality and now a gay icon.

○ While the Queen preferred works by Sir Edwin Landseer like Monarch of Glen, in Europe impressionists like Monet and Toulouse-Lautrec were matched in greatness by the post-impressionists such as Van Gogh, Cezanne and Gauguin.

○ In 1895 Marconi sent a message over a mile by wireless, Rontgen discovered X-rays, and Freud published his first work on psychoanalysis.

○ At the turn of the century the map of the world was dominated by pink, and Victoria ruled over a quarter of the Earth's population.

○ The Whigs had turned into the Liberals, Australia became a Commonwealth, and the Irish were agitating for home rule.

○ In 1901 Victoria died aged 81. No other monarch's name is so synonymous with a particular period in history.

SIR ROBERT PEEL (1788–1850)

Years in office: 1834–5 and 1841–6
Party: Tory
Age when first became PM: 46
Time at Number 10: 5 years, 57 days
Nickname: 'Orange Peel' (because of his anti-Catholic behaviour as a minister in Ireland)

Groomed for stardom by his wealthy mill owner father who told his son: 'If you do not become Prime Minister some day I'll disinherit you.' His government was a milestone for social reform, most famous for introducing the first London police force, nicknamed 'bobbies'. His smile was described as 'the silver plate on a coffin', but he was hugely popular. Died after falling from his horse in Hyde Park's Rotten Row. He was 62. His death plunged the country into mourning.

The Wit and Wisdom

On politics: 'There seems to be very few facts, at least ascertainable facts, in politics.'

'Of all the vulgar acts of Government, that of solving every difficulty that might arise by thrusting the hand into the public purse is the most illusory and contemptible.'

On society: 'The police are the public, and the public are the police.'

'In every village there will arise a miscreant to establish the most grinding tyranny by calling himself The People.'

'Public opinion is a compound of folly, weakness, prejudice, wrong feeling, right feeling, obstinacy and newspaper paragraphs.'

LORD JOHN RUSSELL (1792–1878)

Years in office: 1846–51 and 1865–6
Party: Liberal
Age when first became PM: 53
Time at Number 10: 6 years, 11 days
Nicknames: 'Finality Jack' and 'The Widow's Mite'

Reputation as a weak leader. Fond of younger women. His first wife Adelaide was 15 years his junior. When she died he married Frances who was 23 years younger. They bore him six children. One of his descendants was his grandson, the philosopher Bertrand Russell. Died aged 85.

The Wit and Wisdom

On himself: 'I have made mistakes, but in all I did, my object was the public good.'

On politics: 'If peace cannot be maintained with honour it is no longer peace.'

THE EARL OF DERBY (1799–1869)

Years in office: 1852; 1858–9 and 1866–8
Party: Conservative
Age when first became PM: 52
Time at Number 10: 3 years, 280 days
Nicknames: 'Scorpion Stanley' and 'The Rupert of Debate'

Considered to be the father of the modern Conservative Party. An aristocrat who was very bright. He translated *The Iliad* into blank verse but he had a reputation as a bit of a bore. The regular parties he gave were described as 'dull and depressing as a London fog'. Died aged 70.

The Wit and Wisdom

Describing Earl Russell's foreign policy: 'Meddle and muddle!'

Last words on his deathbed when he was asked how he was: 'Bored to utter extinction.'

Last speech to the House of Lords: 'I am now an old man and like many of your Lordships I have already passed the three score years and ten. My official life is now closed, my political life is nearly so, and, in the course of time, my natural life cannot now be long.'

EARL OF ABERDEEN (1784–1860)

Years in office: 1852–5
Party: Tory
Age when first became PM: 68
Time at Number 10: 2 years, 42 days

Handsome with a mop of dark curly hair just like his cousin Lord Byron, but he was not a philanderer. He was brought down by his handling of the Crimean War and by the fact that he could not handle the strong personalities in his own Cabinet who included Palmerston, Russell and Gladstone. Died aged 76.

The Wit and Wisdom

On himself: 'I do not know how I shall bear being out of office. I have many resources and many objects of interest, but after being occupied with great affairs it is not easy to subside to the level of common occupations.'

VISCOUNT PALMERSTON (1784–1865)

Years in office: 1855–8 and 1859–65
Party: Liberal
Age when first became PM: 71
Time at Number 10: 9 years, 141 days
Nicknames: 'Lord Cupid' and 'Lord Pumicestone'

Charismatic and popular, and at 71 the oldest PM to take up office for the first time. Abrasive, hence his 'Pumicestone' nickname. He was a ladies' man, cited in a divorce case in 1863 when he was in his late seventies. A terrible timekeeper, he even used to keep Queen Victoria waiting. Died aged 81.

The Wit and Wisdom

On his deathbed: 'Die, my dear doctor! That's the last thing I will do.'

On politics: 'The function of Government is to calm rather than to excite agitation.'

'The Schleswig-Holstein question is so complicated only three men in Europe have ever understood it. One is Prince Albert who is dead. The second was a German professor who became mad. I am the third and I have forgotten all about it.'

'Nations have no permanent friends or allies, they only have permanent interests.'

On society: 'What is merit? The opinion one man has of another.'

BENJAMIN DISRAELI (1804–81)

Years in office: 1868 and 1874–80
Party: Conservative
Age when first became PM: 63
Time at Number 10: 6 years, 339 days
Nickname: 'Dizzy'

Only Jewish Prime Minister, with a justly earned reputation for being witty and able. He had a remarkable relationship with Queen Victoria. A clue to that friendship was provided by Disraeli himself when he said: 'Everyone likes flattery, and when it comes to Royalty, you should lay it on with a thick trowel.' He had a longstanding war of words with Gladstone. Died aged 76.

The Wit and Wisdom

'There are three kinds of lies: lies, damn lies and statistics.'

On himself: 'My idea of an agreeable person is a person who agrees with me.'

'Never complain and never explain.'

When he became PM: 'I have climbed to the top of the greasy pole.'

'Life is too short to be little.'

He announced he was going to stand for the constituency of Marylebone and was asked: 'On what do you intend to stand?' Disraeli replied: 'On my head.'

Disraeli wrote to an author who had sent him an unsolicited book: 'Many thanks for your book, I shall lose no time in reading it.'

Gladstone once said to Disraeli: 'I predict, Sir, that you will die either by hanging, or some vile disease.' Disraeli replied: 'That depends, Sir, upon whether I embrace your principles or your mistress.'

'The difference between a misfortune and a calamity is this: If Gladstone fell into the Thames it would be a misfortune. But if someone dragged him out again it would be a calamity.'

He also described Gladstone as: 'A sophistical rhetorician, inebriated with the exuberance of his own verbosity.'

On society: 'As a general rule the most successful man in life is the man who has the best information.'

'Grief is the agony of an instant, the indulgence of grief the blunder of a life.'

'An author who speaks about his own books is almost as bad as a mother who talks about her own children.'

'Ignorance never settles a question.'

'The magic of first love is our ignorance that it can never end.'

'Talk to a man about himself and he will listen for hours.'

'Youth is a blunder, manhood a struggle and old age a regret.'

'Time is the great physician.'

'You know who the critics are? The men who have failed in literature and art.'

'Never apologise for showing feeling, when you do so you apologise for truth.'

Attacking Sir Robert Peel: 'The Right Honourable Gentleman's smile is like the silver fittings on a coffin.'

And again about Sir Robert Peel: 'The Right Honourable Gentleman is reminiscent of a poker. The only difference is that a poker gives off occasional signs of warmth.'

A bore: 'One who has the power of speech but not the capacity for conversation.'

'When a man fell into his anecdotage it was a sign for him to retire.'

After being asked how to handle a woman: 'First of all remember she is a woman.'

On his deathbed: 'I had rather live, but I am not afraid to die.'

Also on his deathbed when told Queen Victoria wished to visit him: 'No it is better not. She would only ask me to take a message to Albert.'

'No man is regular in his attendance at the House of Commons until he is married.'

'A university should be a place of light, of liberty and of learning.'

'Upon the education of the people of this country the fate of this country depends.'

'I hold that the characteristic of the present age is craving credulity.'

'Is man an ape or an angel? Now I am on the side of the angels.'

Of the Marquess of Salisbury: 'He is a great master of gibes, and flouts and jeers.'

'I admit that there is gossip ... But the government of the world is carried on by sovereigns and statesmen, and not by anonymous paragraph writers ... or by the hare-brained chatter of irresponsible frivolity.'

On the Derby: 'The blue ribbon of the turf.'

'The youth of a nation are the trustees of posterity.'

'A protestant, if he wants aid or advice on any matter can only go to his solicitor.'

'When I want to read a novel I write one.'

On being offered a comfy air cushion to sit on: 'Take away that emblem of mortality.'

'I will not go down in history talking bad grammar.' (While correcting proofs of his last Parliamentary speech.)

WILLIAM EWART GLADSTONE
(1809–98)

Years in office: 1868–74; 1880–85; 1886; and 1892–4
Party: Liberal
Age when first became PM: 58
Time at Number 10: 12 years, 126 days
Nickname: 'Grand Old Man' or 'The People's William'

A deeply religious man who brought a high moral tone to politics. He is said to have represented the best qualities of Victorian England but the Queen hated him. She called him 'a half-mad firebrand who addresses me as if I were a public meeting'. Gladstone often walked the streets attempting to persuade prostitutes to reform. He was attacked and injured by a wild heifer, which was later shot dead and its head displayed in a public bar. Died aged 88.

The Wit and Wisdom

On his relations with Queen Victoria: 'What that Sicilian mule was to me, I have been to the Queen.'

On society: 'We look forward to a time when the Power of Love will replace the Love of Power. Then will our world know the blessings of peace.'

'Justice delayed is justice denied.'

'The love of freedom itself is hardly stronger in England than the love of aristocracy.'

On politics: 'Liberalism is trust of the people, tempered by prudence; Conservatism, distrust of people tempered by fear.'

'My mission is to pacify Ireland.'

'We are bound to lose Ireland in consequence of years of cruelty, stupidity and misgovernment and I would rather lose her as a friend than as a foe.'

'You cannot fight against the future. Time is on our side.'

'We have been borne down in a torrent of gin and beer.'

'I would tell them of my own intention to keep my counsel .. and I will venture to recommend them, as an old Parliamentary hand, to do the same.'

On Cross's *Life of George Eliot*: 'It is not a Life at all. It is a Reticence, in three volumes.'

'I will back the masses against the classes.'

'Swimming for his life, a man does not see much of the country through which the river winds.'

On public speaking: 'I absorb the vapour and return it as a flood.'

ROBERT GASCOYNE-CECIL, MARQUESS OF SALISBURY (1830–1903)

Years in office: 1885–6; 1886–92 and 1895–1902
Party: Conservative
Age when first became PM: 55
Time at Number 10: 13 years, 252 days

An icon of traditional, aristocratic Conservatism but a reserved and distant figure more interested in foreign affairs, particularly in Africa, than what was happening in Britain. Against his father's wishes he married Georgina Alderson and was cut off. He was forced to write for newspapers to make a living. But the marriage turned out to be an extremely happy one. The phrase 'Bob's your uncle' began when he gave his nephew the job of Home Secretary. Died aged 73.

The Wit and Wisdom

'English policy is to float lazily downstream occasionally putting out a diplomatic boathook to avoid collisions.'

THE EARL OF ROSEBERY (1847–1929)

Years in office: 1894–5
Party: Liberal
Age when first became PM: 46
Time at Number 10: 1 year, 109 days

At university he had three objects in life: to marry an heiress; to own a racehorse and win the Derby; and to become Prime Minister. He achieved all three but was kicked out of university when he broke the rules to become a racehorse owner. Married Hannah from the fabulously rich Rothschilds who inherited £2 million in cash in 1874. But was reluctant to enter Number 10 when the chance came, longing for a life on the turf instead. He was a chronic insomniac who tried to cure his sleeplessness by driving round London at night in a primrose-coloured coach. He died aged 82.

The Wit and Wisdom

'The British Empire is a Commonwealth of Nations.'

'There are two supreme pleasures in life. One is ideal, the other real. The ideal is when a man receives the seals of office from his Sovereign. The real pleasure comes when he hands them back.'

On his deathbed he asked to hear, for one last time, the *Eton Boating Song.*

EDWARDIAN PRIME MINISTERS: A CLASS ACT!

○ Edward VII finally succeeded his mother but his love of the good life meant he only reigned for nine years and died aged 68.

○ In the fields of science, social reform, politics and the arts, however, there were extraordinary developments at the start of the twentieth century.

○ The first Nobel prizes were awarded, and the suffragette movement began its campaign for women to get the vote.

○ As Rolls Royce manufactured luxury cars, across the Atlantic Henry Ford started production of his Model-T's for the masses.

○ The Tour de France cycling race began in 1903, as the Wright Brothers made their first controlled flight.

○ While San Francisco was destroyed by an earthquake in 1906, there were seismic movements in British politics as the Liberals swept to power but Labour appeared for the first time.

○ The Conservatives split over tariff reform, old age pensions were introduced, and as George V succeeded Edward, he inherited a constitutional crisis.

○ After The Lords rejected Chancellor Lloyd George's 'people's budget' Asquith called for a General Election which resulted in a tie. A second election also produced a hung parliament.

○ In 1911 the Parliament Bill was passed which severely restricted the powers of The Lords, and gave more power to The Commons.

○ Meanwhile Scott died after discovering Amundsen had beaten him to the South Pole, the *Titanic* sank on its maiden voyage, and Einstein put forward his general theory of relativity.

○ The 1914 assassination of Archduke Ferdinand, heir to the Hapsburg throne, in Sarajevo, was the spark which lit the fuse of the First World War.

○ Millions were to die in pointless slaughter in what became known as 'The Great War'.

ARTHUR JAMES BALFOUR (1848–1930)

Years in office: 1902–5
Party: Conservative
Age when first became PM: 53
Time at Number 10: 3 years, 145 days
Nicknames: 'Bloody Balfour'; 'Pretty Fanny' and
'Lisping Hawthorn Bird' (at Cambridge)

He inherited £1 million on his 21st birthday. The first Prime Minister to own a car. He was not considered to be a serious politician, was thought to be just amusing himself as an MP and was not taken seriously. The 'Balfour Declaration' paved the way for the creation of Israel. He never married. He died aged 81.

The Wit and Wisdom

'I am more or less happy when being praised, not very comfortable when being abused, but I have moments of uneasiness when being explained.'

He was far-sighted if fears of global warming prove correct. In 1895 he wrote: 'The energies of our system will decay, the glory of the sun will be dimmed, and the earth, tideless and inert, will no longer tolerate the race which has for a moment disturbed its solitude. Man will go down into the pit and all his thoughts will perish.'

'Nothing matters very much, and very few things matter at all.'

HENRY CAMPBELL-BANNERMAN (1836–1908)

Years in office: 1905–8
Party: Liberal
Age when first became PM: 69
Time at Number 10: 2 years, 122 days
Nickname: 'CB'

Once described as being remembered chiefly as the man about whom all is forgotten, but he ran a strong and efficient government. First really radical leader. Very fond of trees, used to wish 'good morning' to favourites on his regular walks. Utterly devoted to his wife Charlotte whom he referred to in *Rumpole of the Bailey* style as 'the final court of appeal' and 'the Higher Authority'. Heartbroken after her death, his health declined and he died in Downing Street one year later. He died aged 71.

The Wit and Wisdom

On health: 'I am an immense believer in bed, in constantly keeping horizontal. The heart and everything else goes slower, and the whole system is refreshed.'

'Good government could never be a substitute for government by the people themselves.'

On Number 10 where he died in 1908: 'This is a rotten old barrack of a house.'

Last words defiantly: 'This is not the end of me!'

HERBERT HENRY ASQUITH
(1852–1928)

Years in office: 1908–16
Party: Liberal
Age when first became PM: 55
Time at Number 10: 8 years, 244 days
Nickname: 'The sledge hammer'

Introduced taxes on unearned income, helping to pave the way for pensions for the over-seventies. Successfully fought the power of the House of Lords by threatening to create hundreds of Liberal peers if they continued to block his reforms. He was described as 'having a season ticket on the line of least resistance, going wherever the train of events carried him.' He died aged 75.

The Wit and Wisdom

On life: 'Youth would be an ideal state if it came a little later in life.'

On *Yes Minister* style civil servants insisting on three sets of figures about the same event: 'One to mislead the public, another to mislead the Cabinet and the third to mislead itself.'

On politics: 'Our two rhetoricians (Churchill and Lloyd

George) have good brains of different types. But they can only think talking, just as some people can only think writing. Only the salt of the earth can think inside, and the bulk of mankind cannot think at all!'

At the funeral of Bonar Law: 'It is fitting that we should have buried the Unknown Prime Minister by the side of the Unknown Soldier.'

THE WAR YEARS: WIZARDS, BULLDOGS AND CORONERS

○ In 1914 Britannia really did rule the waves, but by the end of the Second World War in 1945 the country was on its knees and the Empire was ready to be disbanded.

○ The huge death toll of the First World War swept away the strict hierarchy of Edwardian Society.

o But many soldiers who returned home expecting a 'land fit for heroes' found only poverty and unemployment instead.

o The Russian Revolution of 1917 booted out the Tsars and ushered in the Communists.

o Labour formed its first Government in 1924 under Ramsay MacDonald, and women got the vote in 1928.

o As silent movies gave way to the 'talkies', Laurel and Hardy, Charlie Chaplin and the Marx Brothers helped the world to laugh. Hollywood became the great entertainment capital, and youngsters flocked to California, hoping to become stars.

o Charles Lindbergh made history becoming the first man to fly solo across the Atlantic in 1927.

o But the 'roaring twenties' ended with the Wall Street Crash, followed by the great depression.

o The Royal Family suffered its greatest crisis with the abdication of Edward VIII in 1936 so that he could marry American divorcee Wallis Simpson.

o Unspeakable horrors were unfolding across Europe as Hitler came to power in Germany, began his extermination of the Jews and precipitated the Second World War.

○ The Battle of Britain was the country's 'finest hour'. But the war might have been lost if Hitler hadn't attacked his ally Russia in 1941, and Japan hadn't destroyed the US Navy at Pearl Harbor.

○ Churchill was the right man to win a war, but at home an exhausted population wanted change, and voted him out in 1945.

DAVID LLOYD GEORGE (1863–1945)

Years in office: 1916–22
Party: Liberal
Age when first became PM: 53
Time at Number 10: 5 years, 317 days
Nickname: 'The Welsh Wizard'

A brilliant man who taught himself with a little help from his village school. His scathing wit made him a dreaded opponent in the House of Commons. Acclaimed in 1918 as the man who won the war. Like Blair, Lloyd George's politics involved a lot of high moral tone, and also like Blair, his government faced serious allegations involving the sale of honours, and he was unmasked as a bit of a bounder and philanderer. He died aged 82.

The Wit and Wisdom

Press Baron Lord Beaverbrook said: 'Lloyd George did not seem to care which way he travelled providing he was in the driver's seat.'

On Armistice Day 1918: 'This is no time for words. Our hearts are too full of gratitude to which no tongue can give adequate expression.'

On politics talking about the House of Lords: 'A body

of five hundred men chosen at random from amongst the unemployed.'

Speaking in 1933 on the future he feared: 'The world is becoming like a lunatic asylum run by lunatics.'

On the end of World War I: 'At eleven o'clock this morning came to an end the cruellest and most terrible war that has ever scourged mankind. I hope we may say that thus, this fateful morning, came to an end all wars.'

At the end of the First World War: 'What is our task? To make Britain a fit country for heroes to live in.'

On politics: 'Every man has a House of Lords in his own head. Fears, prejudices, misconceptions – those are the peers and they are hereditary.'

On Neville Chamberlain: 'He saw foreign policy through the wrong end of a municipal drainpipe.'

On Herbert Samuel (first Jew to lead major political party, the Liberals): 'When they circumcised Herbert Samuel they threw away the wrong bit.'

On politics: 'I am opposed to *Titanic* seamanship in politics and as an old mariner I would not drive the ship on to the ice floes that have drifted into our seas from the frozen wastes of the Tory past.'

'You cannot feed the hungry on statistics.'

'A fully equipped Duke costs as much to keep up as two Dreadnoughts [battleships] and Dukes are just as great a terror, and they last longer.'

On Winston Churchill: 'Winston would go up to his Creator and say that he would very much like to meet His Son, about Whom he had heard a great deal and, if possible, would like to call on the Holy Ghost. Winston loved meeting people.'

On Ramsay MacDonald: 'He had sufficient conscience to bother him, but not sufficient to keep him straight.'

On Field Marshal Lord Haig: 'He was brilliant to the top of his army boots.'

On attempting to negotiate with Irish President Eamon de Valera: 'Like trying to pick up mercury with a fork.'

Before the start of the Second World War: 'If we are going in without the help of Russia we are walking into a trap.'

On the House of Lords and Lord Balfour respectively: 'The trusty mastiff which is to watch over our interests, but which runs away at the first snarl of the trade unions ... A mastiff? It is the Right Honourable Gentleman's poodle.'

Lloyd George wrote his own epitaph, one that might have been adopted by many other politicians: 'Count not my broken pledges as a crime, I MEANT them HOW I meant them, at the time.'

ANDREW BONAR LAW (1858–1923)

Years in office: 1922–3
Party: Conservative
Age when first became PM: 64
Time at Number 10: 209 days
Nickname: 'The Unknown PM'

His nickname belied the real man who was an effective leader and extremely popular on both sides of the House. He had a reputation for honesty and fearlessness. He inherited a large sum of money, which enabled him to go into politics. At that time MPs received no salary, only government ministers were paid. You needed a big income to be even considered for Parliament. He died aged 65.

The Wit and Wisdom

On himself: 'If I am a great man, then a good many of the great men of history are frauds.'

On the proffered resignation of Colonel Seely as War Minister in 1914: 'We have heard of people being thrown to the wolves, but never before have we heard of a man being thrown to the wolves with a bargain on the part of the wolves that they would not eat him.'

On Mussolini in 1922: 'Look at that man's eyes. You will hear more of him later.'

On Churchill: 'I think he has very unusual intellectual ability, but at the same time he seems to have an entirely unbalanced mind, which is a real danger.'

STANLEY BALDWIN (1867–1947)

Years in office: 1923; 1924–9; and 1935–7
Party: Conservative
Age when first became PM: 55
Time at Number 10: 7 years, 82 days

Churchill believed Baldwin's pacifism stance as Hitler began rearming Germany in 1936 gave the German dictator the impression Britain would not fight if attacked. Baldwin was remembered, possibly unfairly, as the man who failed to prevent World War II. Credited with saving the monarchy because of his handling of the abdication of King Edward VIII. He was a cousin of Rudyard Kipling. He died aged 80.

The Wit and Wisdom

As he left Number 10 for the last time in May 1937: 'I am a gentleman at large now!'

On his colleagues in the House of Commons at the end of World War I: 'A lot of hard-faced men who look as if they had done well out of the war.'

On press barons Beaverbrook and Rothermere: 'What the proprietorship of these papers is aiming at is power, and power without responsibility, the prerogative of the harlot through the ages.'

83

On war: 'The only defence is in offence, which means you have to kill more women and children more quickly than the enemy if you want to save yourselves.'

On society: 'There are three groups that no British Prime Minister should provoke: the Vatican, the Treasury and the miners.'

On politics: 'There are three classes which need sanctuary more than others: birds, wild flowers and Prime Ministers.'

On himself: 'I would rather be an opportunist and float than go to the bottom with my principles round my neck.'

Churchill said of him: 'I wish Stanley Baldwin no ill, but it would have been much better had he never lived.'

On his deathbed Baldwin said: 'I am ready!'

JAMES RAMSAY MACDONALD
(1866–1937)

Years in office: 1924 and 1929–35
Party: Labour
Age when first became PM: 57
Time at Number 10: 6 years, 289 days

Lowly lad from Scotland who loved invitations into high society. He was the first genuinely poor man to reach Number 10. He was reluctant to make it his home at first because at that time Prime Ministers were expected to furnish the private apartments, supply all china, glassware and linen as well as paying all household expenses including heating and servants. MacDonald solved the problem of servants by asking his old fisherman friends in his Morayshire home town of Lossiemouth whether they would send their daughters to help the family out. Furniture, furnishing and linen were either borrowed or bought in flea markets. MacDonald, who had never owned a car, continued, at first, to use public transport while living at Number 10. MacDonald was the first Prime Minister to use aeroplanes for official business, flying between Lossiemouth and London in an open cockpit two-seater. He received messages, via a medium, said to come from his dead wife; he replied to some of them. He died aged 71.

The Wit and Wisdom

On Society: 'We hear war called murder. It is not. It is suicide.'

To John Logie Baird, inventor of television, on the delivery of a set to Number 10 in April 1930: 'I felt that the most wonderful miracle is being done under my eye. You have put something in my room which will never let me forget how strange is the world, and how unknown.'

On the abdication of the former King Edward VIII: 'I perhaps am being prejudiced of the immediate harm he (Edward) has done and when the future opens up I shall see that it was all for the good. Still one does not so much respect as be thankful for the tools of providence.' (By 'tools of providence' he meant Wallis Simpson.)

On forming the 1931 national government: 'Tomorrow every Duchess in London will be wanting to kiss me!'

On fears of approaching World War II: 'Let them [France and Germany] especially put their demands in such a way that Great Britain could say that she supported both sides.'

On politics: 'They pushed the nomination down my throat behind my back.'

NEVILLE CHAMBERLAIN (1869–1940)

Years in office: 1937–40
Party: Conservative
Age when first became PM: 68
Time at Number 10: 2 years, 348 days
Nickname: 'The Coroner'

He was completely uncharismatic with a cold manner and grating voice. He believed Hitler was a man of his word. The first time he ever went on a plane was the infamous 1938 flight to see and appease Hitler. He died aged 71.

The Wit and Wisdom

Not a great speech-maker. Aneurin Bevan said: 'Listening to a speech by Chamberlain is like paying a visit to Woolworth's ... everything in its place and nothing above sixpence.'

In 1938 on fear of war: 'In war, whichever side may call itself the victor, there are no winners, but all are losers.'

'How horrible, fantastic, incredible it is that we should be digging trenches and trying on gas-masks here because of a quarrel in a faraway country between people of whom we know nothing.'

87

On hope of peace before World War II: 'This is the second time in our history that there has come back from Germany to Downing Street peace with honour. I believe it is peace for our time. We thank you from the bottom of our hearts. And now I recommend you to go home and sleep quietly in your beds.'

On the declaration of war, September 1939: 'This morning the British Ambassador in Berlin handed the German Government a final note stating that, unless we heard from them by eleven o'clock that they were prepared at once to withdraw their troops from Poland, a state of war would exist between us. I have to tell you that no such undertaking has been received, and that consequently this country is at war with Germany.'

During World War II: 'Whatever may be the reason – whether it was that Hitler thought he might get away with what he had got without fighting for it, or whether it was that after all the preparations were not sufficiently complete – however, one thing is certain: he missed the bus.'

SIR WINSTON LEONARD SPENCER CHURCHILL (1874–1965)

Years in office: 1940–5 and 1951–5
Party: Conservative
Age when first became PM: 65
Time at Number 10: 8 years, 240 days
Nickname: 'Winnie'

He was said to have 'devoted the best years of his life to preparing his impromptu speeches.' Maybe he did, but they are sharp, witty, wounding and sometimes plain vicious, but always straight to the point and elegantly funny. Winston was quite simply the greatest Englishman of his time: a leader in war and peace. He was born in a ladies toilet at Blenheim Palace, when he arrived, unannounced, at a dance. He died aged 90.

The Wit and Wisdom

'I have nothing to offer but blood, toil, tears and sweat.'

To Lady Nancy Astor after she told him that she would poison his coffee if she were his wife. 'Nancy, if I were your husband I would drink it!'

When a woman told Sir Winston that he was drunk,

he retorted: 'I may be drunk, Madam, but in the morning I shall be sober and you will still be ugly.'

On Clement Attlee: 'A sheep in sheep's clothing.'

'A modest man who has much to be modest about.'

'An empty taxi arrived at 10 Downing Street, and when the door was opened, Attlee got out.'

On himself: 'History will be kind to me for I intend to write it.'

'I am always ready to learn although I do not always like being taught.'

'I like pigs. Dogs look up to us. Cats look down on us. Pigs treat us as equals.'

'Why talk with the monkey when you can talk with the organ grinder?'

'I am ready to meet my Maker – but whether my Maker is prepared for the great ordeal of meeting me is another matter.'

'Eating my words has never given me indigestion.'

'I have taken more out of alcohol than alcohol has taken out of me.'

On Neville Chamberlain: 'Mr Chamberlain loves the working man, he loves to see him work.'

On Gladstone: 'Mr Gladstone read Homer for fun, which I thought served him right.'

On Ramsay MacDonald: 'We know that he has, more than any other man, the gift of compressing the largest amount of words into the smallest amount of thought.'

On General Montgomery: 'In defeat unbeatable, in victory unbearable.'

On World War II, about Battle of Britain pilots: 'Never in the field of human conflict was so much owed by so many to so few.'

'Now the enemy [Germany] is busy in Russia is the time to make hell while the sun shines!'

'Now this is not the end. It is not even the beginning of the end, but it is, perhaps, the end of the beginning.'

'You [Hitler] do your worst, and we will do our best.'

'We shall defend our island whatever the cost may be. We shall fight on the beaches, we shall fight on the landing grounds, we shall fight in the fields and in the streets, we shall fight in the hills; we shall never surrender.'

'When I warned them [the French] that Britain would fight on alone whatever they did, their generals told their Prime Minister and his divided Cabinet: "In three weeks England will have her neck wrung like a chicken." Some chicken! Some neck!'

'The Americans will always do the right thing ... after they've exhausted all the alternatives.'

'We should have seen that he [Hitler] risked falling between two stools.'

'When you have to kill a man, it costs nothing to be polite.'

'An Iron Curtain has decended across the continent.'

'During the war I consumed German wine but I excused myself that I was not drinking it but interning it.'

'Jaw jaw not war war.'

'If Hitler invaded hell I would make at least a favourable reference to the devil in the House of Commons.'

On politics: '[a politician requires] the ability to foretell what is going to happen tomorrow, next week, next month and next year. And to have the ability afterwards to explain why it didn't happen.'

'The high belief in the perfection of man is appropriate in a man of the cloth, but not in a Prime Minister.'

His definition of a Parliamentary candidate: 'He is asked to stand, he wants to sit, he is expected to lie.'

The difference between a candidate and an MP: 'One stands for a place – the other sits for it.'

'Headmasters have powers at their disposal with which Prime Ministers have never been invested.'

'Not fit to manage a whelk stall.' (His view of the Labour Party in 1945 after he was removed from office.)

'Politics is like waking up in the morning. You never know whose head you'll find on the pillow.'

'An appeaser is one who feeds a crocodile, hoping that it will eat him last.'

'A fanatic – one who won't change his mind, and can't change the subject.'

'I cannot forecast to you the action of Russia. It is a riddle wrapped in a mystery inside an enigma.'

'The best argument against democracy is a five minute conversation with the average voter.'

'I can think of no better step to signalise the inauguration of the National Health Service than that Aneurin Bevan, who so obviously needs psychiatric attention, should be among the first of its patients.'

'There is no finer investment for any community than putting milk into babies.'

'National compulsory insurance for all classes for all purposes from the cradle to the grave.'

'The empires of the future are the empires of the mind.'

'Men occasionally stumble over the truth, but most of them pick themselves up and hurry off as if nothing had happened.'

'Graham Sutherland's portrait of me makes me look as if I were straining a stool.'

'Scientists should be on tap but not on top.'

'Jellicoe was the only man on either side who could lose the war in an afternoon.'

Winston had a problem when he met Saudi King Ibn Saud for lunch in 1945 and wanted, as usual, to smoke and drink without offending the King's Muslim faith. Churchill said: 'I told him my religion prescribed as an absolute sacred rite smoking cigars and drinking alcohol

95

before, after and, if need be, during all meals and the intervals between them. The outcome? Complete surrender. If only things were so easy for today's politicians.'

George Bernard Shaw sent him tickets for the first night of *St Joan*, 'for yourself and a friend if you have one'. Churchill replied that he could not make the first night but asked instead for tickets for the second night 'if there is one!'

Stepping stark naked from his bath in front of a startled President Roosevelt: 'The Prime Minister has nothing to hide from the President of the United States.'

THE POST-WAR PRIME MINISTERS: YOU'VE NEVER HAD IT SO GOOD!

○ The Atomic bombs on Hiroshima and Nagasaki finally made Japan accept defeat, but also ushered in the nuclear age and the Cold War.

○ America and Russia embarked upon a forty-year arms race, and man for the first time had the power to destroy the earth.

○ Churchill declared an 'Iron Curtain' had descended as The Soviet Union ruled over Eastern Europe, while Korea became the theatre for the ideological battle against Communism.

○ At home Clement Attlee's reforming Labour Government founded the NHS, but couldn't prevent Churchill returning to power one last time.

○ Fifties Britain was still a bleak landscape of bomb sites and queues for rationed food.

○ George VI died in 1952 and was succeeded by a young Elizabeth II. Her Coronation in 1953 was one of the first great televised events shared by the nation.

○ The Suez crisis ruined Anthony Eden's brief premiership, but the world was about to be cheered up by the arrival of rock and roll and Elvis Presley.

○ Rationing was replaced by a consumer boom as technology provided prosperity, and Macmillan declared: 'You've never had it so good.'

○ The new idols were screen rebels like James Dean and Marlon Brando, while in Britain Mods and Rockers met up at seaside resorts for almost choreographed punch-ups.

○ The Berlin Wall divided East and West Germany, the Cuban missile crisis brought the world close to Armageddon, and Yuri Gagarin became the first man to fly into space.

○ A young, Catholic American president, John F Kennedy, promised man would walk on the Moon by the end of the decade, and offered hope for the future. But his assassination still haunts us today.

○ In 1963 Britain shivered in one of its worst ever winters.

○ But four lads from Liverpool were about to bring much-needed relief.

CLEMENT ATTLEE (1883–1967)

Years in office: 1945–51
Party: Labour
Age when first became PM: 63
Time at Number 10: 6 years, 92 days
Nickname: 'Clem'

Voted the most effective Prime Minister of the 20th century although he was quiet, unassuming and loved crossword puzzles. Wounded in action at Gallipoli. He presided over the most radical reforms including the NHS, nationalisation of the Bank of England and heavy industry and the start of National Insurance. Although much that he did was momentous in reshaping Britain, much of what he said was unmemorable, but he ensured that his integrity was absolute. He died aged 84.

The Wit and Wisdom

'Often the experts make the best possible ministers in their own field. In this country we prefer rule by amateurs.'

'The House of Lords is like a glass of champagne, which has stood for five days.'

On himself: 'Few thought he was even a starter. There

were many who thought themselves smarter. But he ended PM, CH and OM. An Earl and a Knight of the Garter.'

'Democracy means government by discussion, but it is only effective if you can stop people talking.'

'[Russian Communism] is the illegitimate child of Karl Marx and Catherine the Great.'

'I think the British have the distinction above all other nations of being able to put new wine into old bottles without bursting them.'

'Politics are too serious a matter to be left to the politicians.'

'Dangerous foreigners begin at Calais and don't stop until you get to Bombay, where they speak English and play cricket.'

On Winston Churchill: 'Fifty per cent of Winston is genius, fifty per cent is bloody fool. He will behave like a child.'

'The press lives on disaster.'

SIR ANTHONY EDEN, LATER EARL OF AVON (1897–1977)

Years in office: 1955–7
Party: Conservative
Age when first became PM: 57
Time at Number 10: 1 year, 279 days

Matinee idol looks and elegantly dressed. Described as the worst Prime Minister since Lord North. Even after the Suez conflict had destroyed his reputation he refused to believe he was wrong. Aneurin Bevan said he was: 'Too stupid to be Prime Minister.' R.A. Butler said of Sir Anthony: 'He was half mad baronet and half beautiful woman.' Eden was a World War I hero who fought in the Somme and won a Military Cross for rescuing a wounded officer. He was a brilliant diplomat as Foreign Secretary, and Churchill was so impressed by him at the height of World War II that he recommended Eden to King George VI as his successor should he himself be killed. Died a saddened, broken man after the failure of his Suez campaign. Died aged 79.

The Wit and Wisdom

On Suez: 'I thought and think that failure to act would have brought the worst of consequences just as I think

103

the world would have suffered less if Hitler had been resisted on the Rhine.'

'We are not at war with Egypt. We are in an armed conflict.'

'If you've broken the eggs you should make the omelette.'

On society: 'Everybody is always in favour of general economy and particular expenditure.'

'Man should be master of his environment, not its slave. This is what freedom means.'

'We best avoid wars by taking physical action to stop small ones.'

'Corruption has never been compulsory.'

On himself: 'I am one of a rare breed of true politicians who definitely say what they may or may not mean with absolute clarity.'

Responding to a question about what effect Joseph Stalin's death would have on international affairs: 'That is a good question for you to ask, not a wise question for me to answer.'

HAROLD MACMILLAN (1894–1986)
(LATER EARL OF STOCKTON)

Years in office: 1957–63
Party: Conservative
Age when first became PM: 62
Time at Number 10: 6 years, 281 days
Nicknames: 'Supermac' and 'Mac the Knife'

He was totally out of touch with the sixties era in which he found himself and had a reputation for being devious and ruthless. Profoundly affected by poverty and hardship in the North East after becoming MP for Stockton-on-Tees. Popular in his first term of office when he presided over a period of prosperity. His second term proved less so with criticism of his handling of the Profumo affair. Died aged 92.

The Wit and Wisdom

On the delights of being Prime Minister: 'Interesting work, fine town house, nice place in the country, servants, plenty of foreign travel.'

'When you're abroad you're a statesman: when you're at home you're just a politician.'

To South Africans: 'The wind of change is blowing

through this continent and whether we like it or not this growth of national consciousness is a political fact.'

On President Kennedy: 'Spending half his time thinking about adultery, the other half about second-hand ideas passed on by his advisers.'

On life: 'If you don't believe in God, all you have to believe in is decency. Decency is very good, better decent than indecent. I don't think it's enough.'

'To be alive at all involves some risk.'

'Tradition does not mean that the living are dead, it means that the dead are living.'

'A man who trusts nobody is apt to be the kind of man no one trusts.'

'No man succeeds without a good woman behind him, wife or mother, if it is both then he is twice blessed indeed.'

On the Profumo affair involving Christine Keeler and Mandy Rice-Davies: 'I was determined that no British government should be brought down by the antics of two tarts.'

'It has been said that there is no fool like an old fool,

except a young fool. But the young fool has first to grow up to be an old fool to realise what a damn fool he was when he was a young fool.'

After General de Gaulle said a very firm '*Non*' to proposed British Common Market entry: 'The French always betray you in the end.'

On Mrs Thatcher's policy of privatisation: 'Like selling the family silver.'

On power: 'Power? It's like a Dead Sea fruit. When you achieve it, there is nothing else.'

On death: 'Memorial services are the cocktail parties of the geriatric set.'

'When the curtain falls, the best thing an actor can do is to go away.'

In 1986 with only weeks to live: 'Sixty-three years ago the unemployment figure [in Stockton-on-Tees] was then twenty-nine per cent. Last November [1986] the unemployment figure was twenty per cent. A sad end to one's life.'

On the Liberals: 'As usual the Liberals offer a mixture of sound and original ideas. Unfortunately none of the sound ideas is original and none of the original ideas is sound.'

107

'Let us be frank about it – most of our people have never had it so good.' Usually paraphrased as 'You've never had it so good.'

'When asked what represented the greatest challenge for a statesman: 'Events, my dear boy, events.'

'We have not overthrown the divine right of kings to fall down for the divine right of experts.'

'I have never found in a long experience of politics, that criticism is ever inhibited by ignorance.'

'Britain's most useful role is somewhere between bee and dinosaur.'

'It's no use crying over spilt summits.'

On Communism: 'Marxism is like a classical building that followed the Renaissance, beautiful in its own way, but incapable of growth.'

'There might be one finger on the trigger, but there will be fifteen fingers on the safety catch.'

To Harold Wilson who had made claims about his childhood saying he had 'no boots to go to school': 'If Mr Wilson did not have boots to go to school, that is because he was too big for them.'

To a fellow Conservative: 'We are Greeks in the Roman Empire. You will find the Americans much as the Greeks found the Romans – a great big, vulgar, bustling people, more vigorous than we are, but also more idle, with more unspoilt virtues but also more corrupt.'

Advice for retiring politicians: 'Don't hang around in the green room after final retirement from the stage.'

'I like to take a Trollope to bed but if one is not available I will settle for a Wodehouse.'

His last words at the age of 92: 'I think I'll go to sleep now.'

SIR ALEC DOUGLAS-HOME (1903–95)

Years in office: 1963–4
Party: Conservative
Age when first became PM: 60
Time at Number 10: 362 days
Nicknames: 'Home Sweet Home' and 'Baillie Vass'
(coined by *Private Eye* after Home's photograph
appeared in the *Aberdeen Evening Express* over the
caption of a baillie (magistrate) called Vass.

Born with a silver spoon in his mouth: heir to 134,000 acres and Scottish coal mines; but with a social conscience. His father taught him to love nature and to be of service to the poor. He renounced his peerage to return to the Commons but he was not a successful PM. He said his short term of office was like Daniel being thrown into the lion's den. He was the only British Prime Minister to play first class cricket, turning out in ten first class matches. He died aged 92.

The Wit and Wisdom

'I would never do anything to deride the profession of politics – although I think it is a form of madness.'

On life: 'It doesn't matter if a cat is black or white, so long as it catches mice.'

On cricket: 'My wife had an uncle who could never walk down the nave of an abbey without wondering whether it would take spin.'

On himself: 'There are two problems in my life. The political ones are insoluble and the economic ones are incomprehensible.'

'It isn't really necessary for a Prime Minister to be popular.'

THE SWINGING SIXTIES TO THE SEQUINNED SEVENTIES

○ The Beatles ushered in the 'Swinging Sixties' and became the most popular entertainment act the world had ever seen.

○ Britain was no longer a mighty military or economic power, but its cultural influence was global.

○ The Rolling Stones, Twiggy, Carnaby Street, the Mini car and the mini-skirt spread the Union Jack across the continents.

o England won the 1966 football World Cup, with Bobby Moore holding aloft the trophy at Wembley.

o A sexual revolution was underway, with the contraceptive pill helping to make casual encounters commonplace. Homosexuality was legalised and divorce and abortion made easier.

o Hippies from San Francisco to Southend preached 'free love' and believed drugs would expand their minds.

o Blacks won rights in America, but the assassinations of Martin Luther King and Robert Kennedy in 1968 meant civil rights came at a cost.

o That same year De Gaulle was nearly toppled by rioting students in Paris, and Soviet troops invaded Czechoslovakia.

o Vietnam was America's greatest burden, but the decade ended in triumph when Neil Armstrong and Buzz Aldrin walked on the Moon in July 1969.

o As colour TV became the norm, Andy Warhol turned a tin of soup into an art-form.

o Germaine Greer wrote *The Female Eunuch* as feminists burned their bras.

o Ted Heath took Britain into the Common Market at the start of 1973 but was brought down at home by the miners.

○ Richard Nixon extricated America from Vietnam but was ruined by the Watergate scandal.

○ And Arab oil producers quadrupled prices overnight sparking an energy crisis. But by the mid-70s Britain had discovered its own 'black gold' in the North Sea.

○ In 1978 Parliamentary debates were broadcast on radio for the first time, but Britain's economy was in a mess with high inflation and industrial unrest. Harold Wilson's successor Jim Callaghan mishandled the 'Winter of Discontent' and by 1979 it was time for a radical change.

HAROLD WILSON (LATER BARON WILSON OF RIEVAULX) (1916–95)

Years in office: 1964–70 and 1974–6
Party: Labour
Age when first became PM: 48
Time at Number 10: 7 years, 279 days

Harold made much of his humble secondary school origins. He even dropped his first name (James) in favour of Harold because it sounded more middle class. As part of his popular 'man of the people' image he denounced Alec Douglas-Home as a 'scion of the effete establishment'. In truth he was a wily, pragmatic tactician who kept his Yorkshire accent and made sure the nation knew his preference was for beer rather than champagne. He died aged 79.

The Wit and Wisdom

'I haven't read Karl Marx. I got stuck on that footnote on page two.'

'A week is a long time in politics.'

'Whichever party is in office, the Treasury is in power.'

'Have you ever noticed how we only win the World Cup under a Labour Government?'

'He who rejects change is the architect of decay.'

'One man's wage rise is another man's price increase.'

'The Labour Party is like a stagecoach. If you rattle along at great speed everybody inside is too exhilarated or too seasick to cause any trouble. But if you stop everybody gets out and argues about where to go next.'

'Every dog is allowed one bite but a different view is taken of a dog that goes on biting all the time.'

To Labour Party Conference, 1962: 'This party is a moral crusade, or it is nothing.'

On the case of Christine Keeler: 'There is something utterly nauseating about a system of society which pays a harlot twenty-five times as much as it pays its Prime Minister, two hundred and fifty times as much as it pays its members of Parliament, and five hundred times as much as it pays some of its ministers of religion.'

On Sir Alec Douglas-Home becoming Prime Minister: 'After half a century of democratic advance, the whole process has ground to a halt with a fourteenth Earl.'

On the so-called 'friendship' between Harold Macmillan and and R.A. Butler: 'Every time Macmillan comes back from abroad, Mr Butler goes to the airport and grips him warmly by the throat.'

'Hence the practised performances of latter-day politicians in the game of musical daggers. Never be left holding the dagger when the music stops.'

On himself: 'I am an optimist, but I'm an optimist who carries a raincoat.'

'Courage is the art of being the only one who knows you're scared to death.'

'I believe the greatest asset a head of state can have is the ability to get a good night's sleep.'

'The main essentials of a successful Prime Minister [are] sleep and a sense of history.'

'If I had the choice between smoked salmon and tinned salmon, I'd have it tinned, with vinegar.'

'The school I went to in the north was a school where more than half the children in my class never had any boots and shoes to their feet. They wore clogs because they lasted longer than shoes of comparable price.'

On death: 'The only human institution which rejects progress is the cemetery.'

On society: 'Everybody should have an equal chance but they shouldn't have a flying start!'

After being hit in the eye by a stink bomb thrown by a schoolboy in 1969: 'With an arm like that he ought to be in the English cricket XI.'

On Tony Benn: 'I have always said about Tony that he immatures with age.'

On the Queen: 'The monarch is a labour-intensive industry.'

'In all our plans for the future we are defining and we are reinstating our Socialism in terms of the scientific revolution. But the revolution cannot become a reality unless we are prepared to make far-reaching changes in economic and social attitudes which permeate our whole system of society. The Britain that is going to be forged in the white heat of the revolution will be no place for restrictive practices.' Usually quoted as the 'white heat of the technological revolution'.

'I get a little nauseated when I hear the phrase "freedom of the press" used as freely as it is: knowing that a large part of our proprietorial press is not free at all.'

'From now on, the pound abroad is worth 14 per cent or so less in terms of other currencies. It doesn't mean, of course, that the pound here in Britain, in your pocket, or purse, or in your bank, has been devalued.'

SIR EDWARD HEATH (1916–2005)

Years in office: 1970–4
Party: Conservative
Age when first became PM: 53
Time at Number 10: 3 years, 259 days
Nicknames: 'The Grocer' and 'The Incredible Sulk'

This former grammar school boy broke the mould of upper class Conservative leaders but had to endure snobbish attacks on his background. His government floundered when his confrontation with trade union power turned into the 'three day week' with the nation sitting in darkness. Hated and constantly attacked Mrs Thatcher. Took Britain into the Common Market in 1973 but seemed totally unaware that his obsession with Europe made him deeply unpopular with many Tories. Remained a bachelor. Died aged 89.

The Wit and Wisdom

On politics: 'If politicians lived on praise and thanks, they'd be forced into some other line of work.'

'The unpleasant and unacceptable face of capitalism.' (The Lonhro affair in the House of Commons.)

'We may be a small island, but we are not a small people.'

'We [the government] are the trade union for pensioners and children, the trade union for the disabled and the sick – the trade union for the nation as a whole.'

After meeting Heinrich Himmler in 1937: 'The most evil man I have ever met.'

On Mrs Thatcher: After his retirement he was often asked to comment on Mrs Thatcher's actions or speeches. His favourite reply: 'I don't know, I'm not a doctor.'

'They made a grave mistake choosing that woman.'

'Whatever the Lady does is wrong. I do not know of a single right decision taken by her.'

'At a photo call, Baroness Thatcher said I should be on her right. I replied that this would be difficult.'

'Rejoice! Rejoice!' (On hearing about Mrs Thatcher's resignation.)

'Do you know what Mrs Thatcher did in her first budget? She introduced VAT on yachts, it somewhat ruined my retirement.'

On Saddam Hussein: 'He is not mad in the least. He is a very astute person, a clever person.'

'Abhorrence of apartheid is a moral attitude not a policy.'

'There are lots of people I've helped get into the House of Commons. Looking at them now, I'm not so sure it was a wise thing to do.'

On himself: 'I have no interest in sailing round the world. Not that there is any lack of requests for me to do so.'

'I am not a product of privilege. I am a product of opportunity.'

JAMES, LATER LORD, CALLAGHAN (1912–2005)

Years in office: 1976–9
Party: Labour
Age when first became PM: 64
Time at Number 10: 3 years, 29 days
Nicknames: 'Big Jim' or 'Sunny Jim'

He clawed his way up the political greasy pole from lowly trade union official and Welsh MP to a place in Harold Wilson's cabinet. He is the only person to have become PM, Chancellor of the Exchequer, Home Secretary and Foreign Secretary. He only became Labour leader after Wilson's shock resignation because he was considered to be the least divisive candidate. His complacent manner and his 'crisis, what crisis?' quip as the country was paralysed by strikes ensured Mrs Thatcher's projection into Number 10. Died aged 92.

The Wit and Wisdom

On society: 'A lie can be half way around the world before the truth has got its boots on.'

'Some people, however long their experience, or strong their intellect, are temperamentally incapable of reaching firm decisions.'

On politics: 'If Labour is dead in Scotland then, from now on, I shall believe in life in the hereafter.'

To Labour supporters at annual Brighton conference: 'Either back us or sack us.'

'I see no signs of mounting crisis.' (When returning from Guadeloupe Summit Conference to find his government in ruins – often misquoted as 'crisis, what crisis?')

'A leader must have the courage to act against an expert's advice.'

'You never reach the promised land. You can march towards it.'

'A leader has to "appear" consistent. That doesn't mean he has to be consistent.'

'I sum up the prospects for 1967 in three short sentences. We are back on course. The ship is picking up speed. The economy is moving. Every seaman knows the command at such a moment. "Steady as she goes".' (Budget speech just before the pound was devalued.)

INTO THE EIGHTIES:
THE LADY'S NOT
FOR TURNING!

○ Grocer's daughter Margaret Thatcher became Britain's first woman Prime Minister in May 1979 and vowed to transform the country.

○ She set about taming the unions, cutting red tape and streamlining industry, but the result was high unemployment and she looked doomed to failure. Riots in Liverpool's Toxteth and London's Brixton highlighted social unrest.

o But in 1982 Argentina's military dictator General Galtieri ordered an invasion of the Falklands, prompting war in the South Atlantic. A determined Thatcher sent a task force to liberate the islands, and the resulting victory made her the most popular Prime Minister since Churchill.

o At home she then saw off the miners who had brought down the previous Conservative government, and survived the 1984 Grand Hotel bombing in Brighton.

o Right-wing US President Ronald Reagan, supported by his soulmate the 'Iron Lady', poured money into defence and made the Soviets realise they could never win the Cold War.

o When Mikhail Gorbachev came to power in 1988 the Soviet economy was in tatters because of the arms race and he faced up to reality. In the space of two years the Berlin Wall came down, Eastern Europe was freed and the Soviet Union began to break up.

o Nations everywhere craved the drug of democracy, but the Tiananmen Square massacre of 1989 crushed the movement in China.

o The growth of globalisation and technological advances like mobile phones and personal computers produced an economic boom.

○ The Stock Market was deregulated in the 1986 'Big Bang' and North Sea oil revenues helped to fuel the recovery as 'Yuppies' flaunted their wealth.

○ The royal family became the tabloids' biggest selling story with fairytale weddings followed by bitter divorces.

○ John Lennon was shot dead outside his New York home in 1980, Bob Geldof turned the world into a global jukebox with his 1985 Live Aid concert to help Africa's starving, and Nelson Mandela was released from prison after more than 25 years to eventually become South African President in 1994.

○ AIDS emerged as a global health threat, a hole appeared in the ozone-layer, and pubs were allowed to open all day.

○ After 11 years, Thatcher was brought down by her own party and replaced by John Major, just in time to preside over the first Gulf War in 1991.

○ Few in the West were aware of the rise of Islamic fundamentalism, but in 1993 a truck bomb exploded under the World Trade Centre in New York. It was a taste of things to come.

MARGARET THATCHER (1925–)
(LATER THE BARONESS THATCHER)

Years in office: 1979–90
Party: Conservative
Age when first became PM: 53
Time at Number 10: 11 years, 209 days
Nicknames: 'The Iron Lady' and 'Attila the Hen'

The grocer's daughter earned her Iron Lady title over her firm stand against the Soviet Union. Her husband Denis described her perfectly when he said: 'I wear the pants in our house but I also wash and iron them.' An unnamed Cabinet colleague said of her: 'The trouble with Margaret is that when she speaks without thinking, she says what she thinks.' There was a huge wave of national patriotism following her successful war in the Falklands. Tony Blair and New Labour followed many of the ideals of Thatcherism.

The Wit and Wisdom

In 1970: 'It will be years before a woman leads the Conservative Party or becomes Prime Minister. I don't see it happening in my time.'

On herself: 'I stand before you tonight in my green chiffon evening gown ... the Iron Lady of the Western World. Me?'

'You turn if you want to – the lady's not for turning.'

'If my critics saw me walking over the Thames they would say it was because I couldn't swim.'

'Any woman who understands the problems of running a home will be nearer to understanding the problems of running a country.'

'I owe nothing to Women's Lib!'

'I'm extraordinarily patient provided I get my own way in the end.'

'Being powerful is like being a lady.'

'We have become a grandmother.'

'The woman's mission is not to enhance the masculine spirit, but to enhance the feminine. Hers is not to preserve a man-made world, but to create a human world by the infusion of the feminine element into all of its activities.'

'I think I have become a bit of an institution – you know, the sort of thing people expect to see around the place.'

'Too many people have been given to understand that

if they have a problem it's the Government's job to cope with it. "I have a problem. I'll get a grant. I'm homeless." They are casting the problem on society and you know there is no such thing as society. There are individual men and women and there are families. No Government can do anything except through people and people must look to themselves.'

In 2006 Baroness Thatcher went with daughter Carol to a street fair in London where she was applauded by an enthusiastic crowd. 'Mum, you are an icon,' said Carol. Baroness Thatcher replied: 'Carol, I think my place in history is assured.'

'Look at a day when you are supremely satisfied at the end. It's not a day when you lounge around doing nothing. It's when you've everything to do and you've done it.'

Unveiling a silicon bronze statue of herself in Parliament in 2007: 'I might have preferred iron – but bronze will do. I hope the head will stay on.' (Referring to a 2002 vandalism of another Thatcher statue, which was decapitated.)

'I could not ask for better company,' she said referring to the statues of Lloyd George, Attlee and Churchill.

'To wear your heart on your sleeve isn't a very good plan. You should wear it inside where it functions best.'

On her husband's death in 2003: 'Being Prime Minister is a lonely job – in a sense it should be – you cannot lead from the crowd. But with Denis I was never alone. What a man! What a husband! What a friend!'

Of her deputy Lord William Whitelaw: 'Every Prime Minister should have a Willie.'

On domesticity: 'Home is where you come to when you have nothing better to do.'

On greed: 'It is not the creation of wealth that is wrong, but love of money for its own sake.'

On society: 'We want a society where people are free to make mistakes, to be generous and compassionate. This is what we mean by a moral society, not a society where the state is responsible for everything and no one is responsible for the state.'

'In my day people would resolve to do something, now [2006] they resolve to be someone!'

'The cocks may crow but it's the hen that lays the egg.'

'No one would remember the Good Samaritan if he'd only had good intentions. He had money as well.'

On terrorism: 'We must try to find ways to starve the

terrorist and the hijacker of the oxygen on which they depend.'

On politics: 'I don't mind how much my ministers talk, as long as they do what I say.'

'Economics are the method, the object is to change the soul.'

'Standing in the middle of the road is very dangerous. You get knocked down by traffic from both sides.'

'In politics if you want anything said, ask a man. If you want anything done ask a woman.'

'Europe will never be like America. Europe is a product of history, America is a product of philosophy.'

'A world without nuclear weapons would be less stable and more dangerous for all of us.'

'I am in politics because of the conflict between good and evil, and I believe that in the end good will triumph.'

Of Mikhail Gorbachev: 'A man we can do business with.'

'Russia are bent on world dominance. The men in the Politburo do not have to worry about the ebb and flow of public opinion. They put guns before butter while we put just about everything before guns.'

135

Denis Thatcher took a group of engineers back to Number 10 for a drink. Mrs Thatcher entered the room and asked who they were. 'Channel Tunnel men,' replied Denis. 'Tunnel! Tunnel! I wanted a bridge!' retorted Mrs Thatcher and promptly left the room.

On the doorstep of Number 10: 'Where there is discord may we bring harmony, where there is error, may we bring truth, where there is doubt, may we bring faith, and where there is despair, may we bring hope.'

SIR JOHN MAJOR (1943–)

Years in office: 1990–7
Party: Conservative
Age when first became PM: 47
Time at Number 10: 6 years, 154 days
Nicknames: 'Mr Interesting' or 'Honest John'

He was described by comedian Jackie Mason as a man who 'makes George Bush seem like a personality'. He really was the man who ran away from the circus to become an accountant and turned into the 'grey man' of Downing Street. A man too decent to be a good Prime Minister as all around him the Conservative Party dissolved in sleaze. Loves cricket. His 'boring' public image got a massive boost when former Tory MP Edwina Currie revealed intimate details of their passionate affair some years after he left office.

The Wit and Wisdom

The late MP Tony Banks said of Major: 'He was so unpopular, if he became a funeral director people would stop dying.'

TV presenter Jeremy Paxman described him as 'flashing the sort of practised smile that comes from a thousand meetings with Prime Ministers of countries most people thought were just anagrams.'

On society: 'Only in Britain could it be thought a defect to be "too clever by half". The probability is that too many people are too stupid by three quarters.'

On politics: 'A consensus politician is someone who does something that he doesn't believe is right because it keeps people quiet when he does it.'

'The politician who never made a mistake never made a decision.'

'The first requirement of politics is not intellect or stamina but patience. Politics is a very long run game and the tortoise will usually beat the hare.'

'If the implication [of his remarks] is that we should sit down and talk with Mr Adams and the Provisional IRA, I can say only that would turn my stomach. I will not talk to people who murder indiscriminately.'

On his political career: 'I am walking over hot coals suspended over a deep pit at the bottom of which are a large number of vipers baring their fangs.'

On becoming Prime Minister: 'I am my own man.'

To a TV interviewer: 'What I don't understand is why such a complete wimp like me keeps winning everything.'

'It is time to return to those core values, time to get back to basics: to self-discipline and respect for the law, to consideration for others, to accepting responsibility for yourself and your family and not shuffling it off on other people and the state.'

'A soundbite never buttered any parsnips.'

Tribute on the death of cricket commentator Brian Johnson: 'Summers simply won't be the same without him.'

NEW MILLENNIUM, NEW LABOUR: THE BLAIR YEARS AND BEYOND

○ After 18 years in power the Conservatives were mired in sleaze and seen as economically incompetent. In May 1997 they were sent packing and Tony Blair's 'New Labour' came to power promising a fresh approach.

○ In fact Chancellor Gordon Brown simply enacted the Tory's spending plans for the next two years, but his masterstroke was to give the Bank of England independence.

○ Blair was thrown in at the deep end with the death of Princess Diana. He dubbed her the 'People's Princess'. It was perhaps the first example of New Labour 'spin', government by headlines orchestrated by former tabloid hack Alastair Campbell.

○ A new Millennium dawned, but current events still brought their mixture of joys and disasters. Dolly the sheep was cloned, Hong Kong was returned to China, Mother Theresa died and 28 people were killed in the Omagh bombing before peace finally came to Northern Ireland.

○ Blair and Brown poured money into health and education, raised revenue by stealth taxes, and began an unprecedented attack on civil liberties with 'Big Brother' intrusions into people's personal lives, banning fox-hunting and smoking in public places. But a decade later there was little to show for it, and crime and immigration were out of control.

○ Gays were given equal rights, President Bill Clinton survived the Monica Lewinsky sex scandal, and Ken Livingstone became Mayor of London.

○ But the events of 11 September, 2001 overshadowed everything when Osama Bin Laden's terrorist group murdered more than 2,500 people in America, flying hi-jacked aircraft into the Twin Towers of the World Trade Centre in New York and the Pentagon in Washington.

- President George Bush and his ally Blair launched a 'war on terror', which led to the invasion of Iraq in 2003 and investigations into Labour's 'dodgy dossiers' on Saddam Hussein's weapons of mass destruction.

- In 2002 the Queen celebrated 50 years on the throne but lost her sister Princess Margaret and the Queen Mum.

- The Euro became the currency of 12 EC countries, but Britain and Denmark stayed out.

- We had foot and mouth, bird flu, and global warming.

- JK Rowling's Harry Potter books became the publishing phenomenon of the decade, while rap videos dominated the pop scene.

- E-mails and mobile phones including cameras and videos became commonplace.

- As Gordon Brown finally replaced Tony Blair, the only certainty was that change will continue.

TONY BLAIR (1953–)

Years in office: 1997–2007
Party: New Labour
Age when first became PM: 43
Time at Number 10: 10 years, 56 days
Nicknames: 'Bambi' and 'George Bush's Poodle'

Began with enormous goodwill and high hopes. Promised to change Britain and reform politics into honest, open government but failed to deliver. Iraq is seen as his Suez disaster – a disastrous legacy of deceit and bad judgement. He was described by former MP Neil Hamilton as 'just like Bill Clinton with his zip done up'. Perhaps significantly, many of his most famous sayings came when he was Labour leader, before becoming Prime Minister.

The Wit and Wisdom

'It is wrong that we spend billions of pounds keeping able-bodied people idle ... we do not want people living in dependency on state hand-outs.' (1994)

'Tough on crime, tough on the causes of crime.' (Describing Labour's Policy in 1994)

'We have no plans to increase tax at all.' (1995)

144

On Tory Prime Minister John Major: 'I lead my party – he follows his.' (1995)

'Ask me my three main priorities for government, and I tell you: education, education and education.' (1996)

'My project will be complete when the Labour party learns to love Peter Mandelson.' (1996)

'I can't stand politicians who wear God on their sleeves.'

'At the time of the election, there will just be one thousand days to the new millennium – a thousand days to prepare for one thousand years, a moment of destiny for us.' (1996)

To his party conference: 'Seventeen years of hurt. Never stopped us dreaming. Labour's coming home.'

'I know exactly what the British people feel when they see the Queen's head on a £10 note. I feel it too.' (1997)

'The very simple choice that people have is this: 'It is twenty-four hours to save our National Health Service.' (1997 election campaign)

'I give you this pledge. Every area of this government's policy will be scrutinised to see how it affects family life.' (1997)

'Our armed services should not be subject to a lack of coherent strategy and piling on of new demands.' (1997)

And in his first month of office: 'Mine is the first generation able to contemplate the possibility that we may live our entire lives without going to war or sending our children to war.' (Blair went on to order British forces into battle five times in his first six years in power.)

On his first day in office: 'A new dawn has broken, has it not?' (May 2 1997)

Being humble: 'We are not the masters now. The people are the masters. We are the servants of the people.' (May 1997)

Paying tribute to Diana, Princess of Wales, after her death: 'She was the people's princess and that is how she will stay, how she will remain in our hearts and minds forever.'

Apologising for mishandling the donation of £1 million to Labour by Formula One boss Bernie Ecclestone: 'I think most people who have dealt with me, think I'm a pretty straight sort of guy and I am.'

'We have to be very careful that we are purer than pure.' (1998)

147

Arriving in Belfast for talks leading to the Good Friday agreement: 'A day like today is not a day for sound-bites, really. But I feel the hand of history upon our shoulders, I really do.'

'The Press is a tiger and whether you like it or not, in politics you are put astride it.'

On his barrister wife Cherie: 'She was always a much better lawyer than I was.'

In 1999: 'I bear the scars on my back after two years in government.'

On the rigours of the job: 'I don't ever stop being Prime Minister.'

On Deputy PM John Prescott: 'John is John and I'm lucky to have him as my deputy.'

'It's not a burning ambition for me to make sure that David Beckham earns less money.'

On 11 September, 2001: 'As for those that carried out these attacks, there are no adequate words of condemnation. Their barbarism will stand as their shame for all eternity. We will not rest until this evil is driven from our world.'

In one of his conference speeches: 'The state of Africa is a scar on the conscience of the world.'

148

On Saddam Hussein's alleged weapons of mass destruction: 'His military planning allows for some of the WMD to be ready within forty-five minutes of an order to use them.'

Before the Commons Iraq vote in 2002: 'This is not the time to falter. This is the time for this house to give a lead.'

In December 2002 he was treated for a heart scare but said: 'My health is absolutely fine – I'm feeling great.'

In September 2003 he told the Labour conference: 'I've not got a reverse gear.'

During a Commons debate in January 2004: 'The allegation that I or anyone else lied to this House or deliberately misled the country by falsifying intelligence on WMD is itself the real lie.'

Before his third election triumph: 'If I am elected, I would serve a full third term. I do not want to serve a fourth term – I don't think the British people would want a Prime Minister to go on that long.'

After London won the 2012 Olympics: 'It's not often in this job that you punch the air and do a little jig and embrace the person next to you.'

The celebrations were cut short by the London bombings the next day, which became known as 7/7. He said of them: 'It's a very sad day for the British people but we will hold true to the British way of life.'

On out-voted plans to detain terror suspects for up to 90 days without trial: 'Sometimes it is better to lose and do the right thing than to win and do the wrong thing.'

In 2006 Michael Parkinson asked about the role of his Christian faith in deciding to invade Iraq. He replied: 'You realise that judgement is made by other people – and if you believe in God, it's made by God as well.'

On Iraq: 'This is not a clash between civilisations. It is a clash about civilisation.'

On the cash for honours probe: 'Nobody in the Labour party to my knowledge has sold honours or sold peerages.'

In September 2006: 'I would have preferred to do this in my own way, but, as has been pretty obvious from what many of my Cabinet colleagues have said earlier in the week, the next party conference in a couple of weeks will be my last as party leader.'

At that conference: 'The truth is you can't go on forever.'

On his successor: 'New Labour would never have happened, and three election victories would never have been secured, without Gordon Brown. He is a remarkable man.'

On his wife's view of Brown: 'At least I don't have to worry about her running off with the bloke next door!'

In his last year, 2007: 'The manner of the execution of Saddam was completely wrong.'

After being interviewed by police on the cash for honours scandal: 'I'm not going to beg for my character.'

On 10 May he announced his resignation saying: 'I ask you to accept one thing. Hand on heart, I did what I thought was right.'

'This is the greatest nation on earth.'

'I give my thanks to you, the British people, for the times I have succeeded, and my apologies for the times I have fallen short.'

GORDON BROWN